BABY BLUES®

BY RICK KIRKMAN / JERRY SCOTT

McGraw Hill

New York   Chicago   San Francisco   Lisbon   London   Madrid   Mexico City
Milan   New Delhi   San Juan   Seoul   Singapore   Sydney   Toronto

The *McGraw·Hill* Companies

Library of Congress Cataloging-in-Publication Data

Kirkman, Rick.
    Baby blues / by Rick Kirkman, Jerry Scott.
        p.   cm.
    Originally published: Chicago : Contemporary books, 1991.
    ISBN 0-8092-3996-5
    I. Scott, Jerry, 1955–.   II. Title.
PN6728.B25K57   1997
741.5'73—dc21   97-19719
                                 CIP

To Kim,
who understands where the words come from.
J.S.

For Sukey, my funnier half, and the girls,
who at age 18 will owe us 39,420 hours of sleep
(but who's counting?)
Thanks to Dr. Clara August, John Irving & Garp.
R.K.

25 26 27 28 29 30 31 32 33 34 35 36 37 38 39   BAH/BAH   0 9 8

ISBN-13: 978-0-8092-3996-2
ISBN-10:   0-8092-3996-5

McGraw-Hill books are available at special quantity discounts to use as premiums and sales promotions, or for use in corporate training programs. For more information, please write to the Director of Special Sales, Professional Publishing, McGraw-Hill, Two Penn Plaza, New York, NY 10121-2298. Or contact your local bookstore.

This book is printed on acid-free paper.

Foreword

Treasure this book. It contains the first year of what I hope will be many years of "Baby Blues"—and it's going to be hard to keep it intact. Every instinct will tell you to grab your scissors and start cutting out strips to send to friends and relatives. You'll fling the scissors aside and start ripping out whole pages to plaster on the refrigerator. Finally, you'll gather up all the little scraps you've pulled out and try to glue the whole book into your own baby's baby book, even if—like me—you don't actually have a baby yet.

And that's the most remarkable thing. With just the right combination of warmth, charm, and total irreverence, Rick Kirkman and Jerry Scott have created a glimpse at a modern relationship that's true enough to make us laugh even if we aren't going through exactly what Darryl, Wanda, and Zoe are going through.

What woman hasn't felt the urge to reach across the breakfast table and squash half a grapefruit over her beloved sweetheart's self-righteous nose? What man hasn't professed his sorrow about being unable to be home in times of crisis and then secretly shrieked for joy because he can escape to the office? What mature, responsible adult hasn't anticipated a visit from Mom and Dad with an equal measure of joy and horror?

Like most of my favorite kind of writing, "Baby Blues" confirms my fears that men and women come from different planets while simultaneously fueling my optimism that we can find a way to like each other anyway.

Because this book starts at the beginning of Zoe's life, we get to watch a couple evolve into a real family. And while we know the anxieties are as old as Great-Grandma, we also know we're seeing solutions that only truly enlightened, evolved parents of the nineties could hit upon: Darryl trying to keep a diaper shut with Post-It Notes . . . Wanda videotaping Darryl pretending to be the baby when the real baby won't perform on tape . . . the baby-sitter running from the home screaming out that she's going to have her tubes tied.

But to me the real beauty of this comic strip is that it reflects exactly what people feel: a jumble of love, angst, insecurity, and hopefulness that's as present when Wanda snarls, "Eat diapers and die" as it is when she looks at her family all packed up for an outing and sighs, "We've not only become parents, we've become nerds." Jerry and Rick never take the easy way out; they're willing to dig beneath the layers of surface jokes they *could* make, in order to get to the simple, honest, real-life moments we need to be able to laugh at most.

I probably look more like Wanda slumped against the bathroom mirror as she starts seeing her mother's face instead of her own . . . but when I read "Baby Blues," I feel more like Darryl when, scrunched up in a blissfully perfect moment, he silently cheers, "YES!!"

Cathy Guisewite

BABY BLUES®

BY RICK KIRKMAN / JERRY SCOTT

Wanda in labor.

DAY 1.

NOW WHAT?

NOW WHAT?

IT'S A GIRL

CON-GRATS

NOW WHAT?

WITH THE NEW BABY NOW AT HOME, DARRYL AND WANDA BEGIN TO ASK THEMSELVES THE IMPORTANT QUESTIONS:

EDITOR'S NOTE: DARRYL & WANDA (SHOWN HERE) HAVE JUST SPENT THE FIRST 24 HOURS AT HOME ALONE WITH THEIR NEW BABY, ZOE.

EDITOR'S NOTE: NEED WE SAY MORE?

KIRKMAN & SCOTT

WHO DO YOU THINK SHE LOOKS LIKE... ME OR YOU?

YOU AND BABY

BLOTCHY SKIN, PUFFY EYES, FAT CHEEKS, CRINKLED FACE...

KIRKMAN & SCOTT

OH, I THINK SHE LOOKS LIKE YOU.

OKAY, LET'S SEE IF I CAN GET THIS RIGHT...

IS IT **WASH**, POWDER, LOTION, OR **LOTION**, WASH, POWDER OR **WASH**, LOTION, POWDER, OR....

KIRKMAN & SCOTT

MAYDAY! MAYDAY!

DARRYL SOLOS

8

Even though she knows it's no big deal, Wanda's self-consciousness about breast-feeding is evident.

11

BABY BLUES®

BY RICK KIRKMAN / JERRY SCOTT

EVERYTHING'S FINE, MOM.

FOR JUST GIVING BIRTH A COUPLE OF DAYS AGO, THINGS ARE SURPRISINGLY UNDER CONTROL

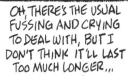

OH, THERE'S THE USUAL FUSSING AND CRYING TO DEAL WITH, BUT I DON'T THINK IT'LL LAST TOO MUCH LONGER...

... HE GOES BACK TO WORK TOMORROW.

KIRKMAN & SCOTT

HOW MANY TIMES HAVE I TOLD YOU NOT TO TOUCH THE PLANTS...

HOW MANY TIMES HAVE I TOLD YOU NOT TO TOUCH THE PLANTS?

YOU'RE GOING TO PUT SOMEONE'S EYE OUT WITH THAT...

YOU'RE GOING TO PUT SOMEONE'S EYE OUT WITH THAT!

JUST WHO DO YOU THINK YOU ARE, BUSTER/SISTER?

JUST WHO DO YOU THINK YOU ARE, BUSTER/SISTER?

BERLITZ FOR MOMS

KIRKMAN & SCOTT

LOOK! IT'S GOT 100 WATTS PER CHANNEL, A GRAPHIC EQUALIZER, DIGITAL DISPLAY, AND SURROUND-SOUND WITH TITANIUM-DOMED TWEETERS! WHAT DO YOU SAY?

BABY MONITORS DON'T NEED TITANIUM-DOMED TWEETERS

HOME ELECTRONICS

KIRKMAN & SCOTT

IT'S NOT JUST A BABY MONITOR—IT'S A LIFESTYLE!

IT'S NOT JUST A BABY MONITOR—IT'S A LIFESTYLE!

14

I GOTTA LOSE WEIGHT!

SOMETHING'S WRONG WITH THESE PANTS...

THE DIFFERENCE BETWEEN MEN AND WOMEN.

KIRKMAN & SCOTT

PHTTHT!

WITH EVERY PASSING NIGHT, WANDA'S SLIGHT RESEMBLANCE TO KATHLEEN TURNER SEEMED TO GROW FAINTER AND FAINTER.

KIRKMAN & SCOTT

IT'S FOURTH & TEN, BUT THE RAMS ARE GONNA GO FOR IT...

DARRYL, WOULD YOU DO ME A FAVOR? I HAVE TO GO TO THE STORE...

OH, NO!

WOULD YOU MIND PARENTING ZOE FOR ME?

HUH? OH, SURE!

KIRKMAN & SCOTT

WHEW! FOR A MINUTE THERE, I THOUGHT SHE WAS GOING TO ASK ME TO **BABYSIT!**

BABY BLUES®

BY RICK KIRKMAN / JERRY SCOTT

Chapter 3
COLIC

How your parents get even with you.

I SHOULD HAVE KNOWN.

IF GRANDMAS RULED THE EARTH.

YOU KNOW, WANDA, IT'S JUST STARTING TO HIT ME THAT WE'RE ACTUALLY A FAMILY, NOW

HERE WE ARE AT HOME, JUST YOU, ME AND OUR OWN...

CRAAH!!

...AIR RAID SIREN.

I'M LOOKING FORWARD TO EVERYTHING...THE BABY'S FIRST STEPS, HER FIRST WORDS, LEARNING TO RIDE A BIKE, GOING ON CAMPING TRIPS...

SO DO SOMETHING ALREADY!!

3:05 PM SATURDAY. ZOE'S UMBILICAL CORD FALLS OFF.

HERE. TAKE THIS.

3:06 PM SATURDAY. WANDA LOCATES THE PEPTO BISMOL.

HERE. TAKE THIS.

KIRKMAN & SCOTT

For Wanda, getting her body back into shape after the baby would be a breeze compared to getting her body into the leotard...

WHO IS THIS CUTIE WOOTIE POOTIE?

WHY, IT'S DADDY'S WIDDLE GIRL! ARE YOU DADDY'S WIDDLE GIRL?

YES YOU ARE!

BLORP!

DID I SAY "DADDY'S WIDDLE GIRL"? I MEANT "MOMMY'S WIDDLE GIRL...

NICE TRY.

KIRKMAN & SCOTT

WHEN IT COMES TO LETTING OTHER PEOPLE HOLD ZOE, DARRYL AND WANDA LET ONLY EXPERIENCED PARENTS WORK WITHOUT A NET.

KIRKMAN & SCOTT

It's a girl! She's 3 weeks old. Yes, she is cute, isn't she?

DARRYL LOSES PATIENCE WITH CHATTY CLERKS.

PAMPIES

KIRKMAN & SCOTT

24

ZOE'S FIRST SHOT.

THE WAY IT USED TO BE...

THE WAY IT IS.

SINGLE

MARRIED

PARENT

COFFEE TABLE EVOLUTION.

KIRKMAN & SCOTT

KIRKMAN & SCOTT

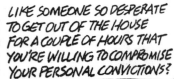

WHAT'S THIS?

My Child's First Year: A Journal by Darryl

Jan. 7, 1990
Day One:
Busy day. Up all night, housework all day. Zoe didn't sleep well.

THAT'S SO SWEET.

Day Two: See Day One.
Day Three: See Day One.
Day Four: See Day One.
Day Five: See Day One.
Day Six: See Day One...

FLIP FLIP FLIP FLIP FLIP FLIP FLIP

YES, HELLO. I WAS WONDERING WHAT YOU CHARGE FOR BABYSITTING?

IT'S FIVE BUCKS AN HOUR FOR THE AVERAGE KID, BUT YOURS WILL RUN AT LEAST THIRTY.

I DIDN'T REALIZE THAT "DEGREE OF DIFFICULTY" WAS A FACTOR.

WAAAAAAA

TWELVE HOURS OF NONSTOP CRYING! WHAT ARE WE GOING TO DO?

I'VE GOT AN IDEA... LET'S TRY SWADDLING HER.

WAAAA AAAA

WHAT'S THAT?

YOU WRAP THEM UP IN A BLANKET REAL SNUGLY TO KEEP THEIR ARMS AND LEGS FROM MOVING AROUND, AND IT RELAXES THEM.

WA WEH WEH

SNIFF SNIFF

I THINK SHE LOOKS SO CUTE.

I THINK SHE LOOKS LIKE A BURRITO.

BABY BLUES

by RICK KIRKMAN / JERRY SCOTT

WE DIDN'T START OUT TIRED
(SUNG TO THE TUNE OF BILLY JOEL'S "WE DIDN'T START THE FIRE")

BABY POWDER, BABY OIL,
RUBBER NIPPLES ON THE BOIL.
PACIFIER, VAPORIZER,
DOCTOR SPOCK IS BACK!

CHANGING TABLE, COTTON DIAPERS,
PAMPERS, HUGGIES, BABY WIPERS,
MIDNIGHT FEEDINGS, SUNRISE GREETING,
ARE WE HAVING FUN?

BASSINET, LAYETTE,
MASTERCARD JUST HAD A FIT.
BREAST FEEDING, BABY GNAWS,
TENDER NIPPLES, NURSING BRAS.

SOFT SPOT, CRADLE CAP,
CRANKY KID, I NEED A NAP!
HOUSECLEANING! INTERRUPTIONS!
NEVER GONNA GET DONE!

(CHORUS)
WE DIDN'T START OUT TIRED.
BUT WE THINK THAT MAYBE
WE CAN BLAME THE BABY.

WE DIDN'T START OUT TIRED.
IT SEEMS DIABOLIC
BUT IT'S PROB'LY COLIC.

TINY FINGERS, LITTLE TOES,
DIAPER RASH AND RUNNY NOSE.
BABY'S SHRIEKING, MILK IS LEAKING.
FIGURE IS SHOT!

PLAYPEN IN THE DEN,
BABY'S SLEEPING, AMEN!
PHONE RINGS, BELL DINGS,
IT MUST BE A PLOT.

COLIC, MYLICON,
WHERE THE HECK IS BRAZELTON?
CAMOMILE, FENNEL TEA,
DOUBLE SCOTCH FOR YOU AND ME.

WHITE NOISE, TAKE A RIDE,
VACUUM CLEANER, ALL TRIED!
ZOMBIE EYES, LULLABIES,
SINGING 'TIL WE'RE CROSS-EYED!

(CHORUS)
WE DIDN'T START OUT TIRED.
BUT WE THINK THAT MAYBE
WE CAN BLAME THE BABY.

WE DIDN'T START OUT TIRED.
BUT FOR THIS LITTLE ONE
OUR LOVE GOES ON AND
ON, AND ON...

(WITH APOLOGIES TO BILLY JOEL)

KIRKMAN & SCOTT

CARDINAL RULE OF FATHERHOOD: ALWAYS WAIT UNTIL YOU'RE OUT OF THE HOUSE TO APPEAR HAPPY TO GO TO WORK.

KIRKMAN & SCOTT

SHE'S SO INNOCENT. SHE'S SO BEAUTIFUL.

HER MIND IS TOTALLY OPEN AND FREE. SHE'LL ACCEPT WHATEVER WE TELL HER WITH COMPLETE TRUST AND FAITH.

KIRKMAN & SCOTT

DADDY IS A GENIUS... DADDY IS A GENIUS...

HI, HONEY. WHAT'S THE MATTER? ARE YOU HUNGRY AGAIN?

HOW ABOUT SOME FAST FOOD? DOES THAT SOUND GOOD? OKAY, LET'S GO FOR A RIDE.

BBBBBBBBB

WE'RE IN LUCK. I THINK I SEE A DRIVE-THRU.

KIRKMAN & SCOTT

YOU'RE AMAZING, DARRYL.

YOU HAVE A NEW BABY AT HOME... YOU GET LITTLE OR NO SLEEP,...AND YOU STILL MANAGE TO PUT IN EIGHT OR TEN HOURS A DAY AT THE OFFICE.

I DON'T KNOW HOW YOU DO IT, MAN.

ZZZ.

I SURE HOPE I'M A GOOD FATHER.

OF COURSE YOU'RE A GOOD FATHER.

BUT I DON'T WANT TO BE JUST A GOOD FATHER. I WANT TO BE A GREAT FATHER! CREATIVE! AGELESS! AN ICON!

I WANT TO BE THE MICK JAGGER OF FATHERHOOD!

RRIPP!

THE WHAT?!

FIGURATIVELY SPEAKING...

THIS IS MY LITTLE GIRL. HER NAME IS ZOE. WOULD YOU LIKE TO SAY "HI" TO HER?

NO!!

WANDA FINDS OUT WHAT SHE HAS TO LOOK FORWARD TO A COUPLE OF YEARS FROM NOW.

BABY BLUES®

RICK KIRKMAN BY JERRY SCOTT

DESPITE THE ENORMOUS STRESS OF CARING FOR HER NEWBORN, THE ANGELIC FACE OF HER CONTENTED CHILD MAKES WANDA THINK WISTFULLY ABOUT HAVING ANOTHER BABY RIGHT AWAY.

SLAPPITY SLAPPITY SLAPPITY SLAP!

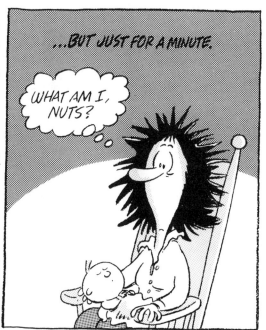

...BUT JUST FOR A MINUTE.

WHAT AM I, NUTS?

DISPOSABLE DIAPERS NOW MAKE UP 2 PERCENT OF ALL THE TRASH IN OUR LANDFILLS!

ENVIRONMENT! BIODEGRADABLE! CRISIS!

IT'S UP TO US TO CHANGE THE WORLD!

I DON'T WANT TO CHANGE THE WORLD... I JUST WANT TO CHANGE MY BABY!

THAT WOMAN ALL BUT ACCUSED ME OF DESTROYING THE PLANET BECAUSE I BOUGHT A BOX OF DISPOSABLE DIAPERS!

SHE'S CRAZY!

THEY CAN'T BE THAT BAD.

IT'S NONE OF HER BUSINESS WHAT I BUY!

YOU'RE RIGHT!

YOU'RE RIGHT!

YOU'RE RIGHT!

IF I'M SO RIGHT, WHY DO I FEEL SO GUILTY?

WE ARE SOCIALLY RESPONSIBLE PEOPLE...

WE DON'T SMOKE, WE RECYCLE ALUMINUM AND NEWSPAPER, WE USE ROLL-ON DEODORANT, AND WE GIVE MONEY TO GREENPEACE.

WE REFUSE TO FEEL GUILTY FOR USING DISPOSABLE DIAPERS, SO JUST CUT US SOME SLACK!!

KIRKMAN & SCOTT

DARRYL, PLEASE...

PAPER OR PLASTIC?

WHAT ARE YOU, SOME KIND OF A WISE GUY!?

THIS DISPOSABLE DIAPER CONTROVERSY IS REALLY BOTHERING ME. DO YOU THINK WE SHOULD USE COTTON DIAPERS ON ZOE?

I DON'T KNOW. HOW DO THEY WORK?

BASICALLY THE SAME AS DISPOSABLE, BUT INSTEAD OF THROWING THE DIRTY ONES AWAY, YOU SWISH THEM AROUND IN THE TOILET WITH YOUR HANDS AND STORE THEM IN A HAMPER UNTIL YOU WASH THEM.

NO. **SERIOUSLY,** HOW DO THEY WORK?

KIRKMAN & SCOTT

STILL THINKING ABOUT THE BIG DIAPER DEBATE?

YEAH. I FIGURED THE FAIREST THING TO DO WAS WRITE DOWN THE STRONG POINTS OF BOTH TYPES AND COMPARE LISTS.

CLOTH DIAPERS
Environmentally Sound
Reusable
Don't jam landfills
Soft on baby
Multi-use
Cheaper than Disposables
Traditional

DISPOSABLE DIAPERS
Don't have to put your hand in the toilet

KIRKMAN & SCOTT

SO, WHAT DO YOU THINK?

NO CONTEST.

DISPOSABLE BY A MILE.

KIRKMAN & SCOTT

WAAAAA

INCREDIBLE COINCIDENCE OR DIABOLICAL SCHEME?

WAAA

THE MIDNIGHT FEEDING:

PRO
WANDA DOESN'T HAVE TO TAPE "LATE NIGHT WITH DAVID LETTERMAN" NOW.

CON
NOTHING IS FUNNY AT MIDNIGHT ANYMORE.

BITE IT, DAVE...

AND OUR NUMBER ONE REASON... JUST BECAUSE HE LIKES THE WAY IT...

KIRKMAN & SCOTT

ACCORDING TO THIS STUDY, IT NOW COSTS $150,000 TO RAISE A CHILD TO AGE 18.

WOW!

AND THAT DOESN'T INCLUDE COLLEGE! ADD $77,000 FOR FOUR YEARS AT AN IN-STATE PUBLIC UNIVERSITY!

THAT'S SCARY.

KIRKMAN & SCOTT

THAT'S OUTRAGEOUS!

THAT'S $27,750 A POUND!

WAAAAA!

YOU & BABY

LET'S SEE...WE CHANGED YOU, POWDERED YOU, FED YOU, BURPED YOU, CUDDLED YOU, SANG TO YOU, CHECKED YOUR TEMPERATURE...

WAAAA WAAAA

YOU & BABY

WAAA

ZOE, I'M AFRAID THIS CRYING IS TOTALLY UNAUTHORIZED.

WAAA

KIRKMAN & SCOTT

BABY BLUES

BY RICK KIRKMAN / JERRY SCOTT

KIRKMAN & SCOTT

43

44

SO WHAT SEEMS TO BE THE PROBLEM?

TIREDNESS... LISTLESSNESS... CRANKINESS...

NO, I MEAN THE BABY.

OH, THE SNIFFLES.

ZZZZ

I'D LIKE TO GIVE ZOE A PRESCRIPTION FOR SOME DROPS THAT SHOULD HELP HER GET OVER THIS.

IF YOU DON'T MIND, WE'D RATHER NOT GIVE ZOE ANYTHING. WE WANT TO RAISE HER WITH AS FEW MEDICATIONS AS POSSIBLE.

IT'LL MAKE HER SLEEP THROUGH THE NIGHT.

YOU'VE GOT YOURSELF A DEAL.

BABIES ARE SO AMAZING!

THE TINY TOES... THE TINY FEET... THE TINY FINGERS... THE TINY HANDS...

I KNOW, SHE'S SO DELICATE.

NELICATE? 'AVE YOU ZEEN DIS KID'S GRIP?

HAVE YOU NOTICED THAT ZOE TENDS TO SPIT UP ON ME A LOT MORE THAN SHE DOES ON YOU?

IT'S JUST YOUR IMAGINATION.

NO! SERIOUSLY! AND SHE ALWAYS DOES IT WHEN I'M DRESSED TO GO SOMEPLACE!

SHE SPITS UP ON ME, TOO, YOU KNOW.

BLORP!

YEAH, BUT YOU DON'T HAVE TO PUT ON A RAINCOAT EVERY TIME YOU WANT A HUG.

KIRKMAN & SCOTT

OOPSIE! WOOPSIE! DOOPSIE!

DARRYL! BE CAREFUL! YOU'LL MAKE HER SICK!

DON'T BE SILLY! SHE...

...LIKES IT.

KIRKMAN & SCOTT

UH-OH... WHERE'S THE DIAPER?

BLORP!

SHE SPIT UP ON YOU AGAIN??

YEAH... I'M KIND OF GETTING USED TO IT.

IT'S JUST HER WAY OF SAYING THAT SHE LOVES HER DADDY!

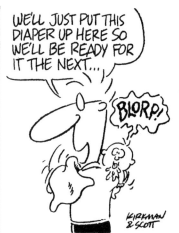

WE'LL JUST PUT THIS DIAPER UP HERE SO WE'LL BE READY FOR IT THE NEXT...

BLORP!

KIRKMAN & SCOTT

47

48

THIS IS A LAMP. IT GOES ON AND OFF. ON AND OFF.

CLICK! CLICK! CLICK! CLICK!

THIS IS YOUR MOMMY. SHE GOES HAPPY, SAD. HAPPY, SAD.

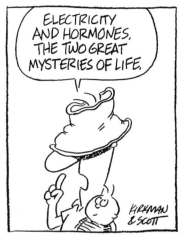

ELECTRICITY AND HORMONES, THE TWO GREAT MYSTERIES OF LIFE.

KIRKMAN & SCOTT

HUNH-HUH-HWAAAAAA!

I'LL GET HER.

THANKS.

BUT BE CAREFUL. LAST TIME YOU GOT UP, YOU STUBBED YOUR TOE RAN INTO THE DOOR AND BANGED YOUR KNEE ON THE COFEEE TABLE.

DON'T WORRY, I'VE GOT IT COVERED.

KIRKMAN & SCOTT

FAST CHECK
15 ITEMS & LESS
CASH & CHECKS

EXPRESS CHECK
5 ITEMS & LESS
CASH ONLY

WARP CHECK
NO LIMIT
CRANKY
BABIES ONLY

KIRKMAN & SCOTT

«CLICK!»

LET'S SEE... I LOCKED ALL OF THE DOORS AND WINDOWS, CHECKED THE DEAD BOLTS, TURNED ON THE PORCH LIGHT AND ARMED THE BURGLAR ALARM.

FOOMP! FOOMP!

MAKES YOU FEEL SECURE, DOESN'T IT?

KIRKMAN & SCOTT

DARRYL, WANDA, NORM AND CINDY DECIDE TO SPEND AN ENTIRE EVENING DISCUSSING ANYTHING BUT CHILDREN.

KIRKMAN & SCOTT

LISTEN TO THIS... People with radio scanners are picking up the signals from baby monitors and listening in on families!

...Some scanners can pick up conversations up to a half-mile away!

THAT'S RIDICULOUS!

I DON'T BELIEVE A WORD OF IT!

THEY EXAGGERATE.

BABY BLUES®

BY RICK KIRKMAN / JERRY SCOTT

HOW MANY WILL BE TRAVELING TODAY?

THREE, WE'RE GOING TO GRANDMA'S HOUSE.

ANY CARRY-ON LUGGAGE?

WELL, THERE'S THE CAR SEAT BUT SHE'LL BE SITTING IN THAT.

IS THAT ALL?

JUST THAT AND THE DIAPER BAG.

COMIN' THROUGH!

KIRKMAN & SCOTT

LADIES AND GENTLEMEN, WE'D LIKE TO START BY PRE-BOARDING PASSENGERS TRAVELING WITH SMALL CHILDREN.

GATE 12

I LOVE THIS. NO STANDING IN LINE... NO SHOVING IN THE AISLES...

THANKS TO ZOE HERE, WE GET TO JUST STROLL BY EVERYBODY ELSE LIKE WE OWN THE PLACE!

KIRKMAN & SCOTT

HOW MANY CHILDREN?

THIS ONE AND THE BIG, DOPEY ONE BEHIND ME.

PHTTHT!

IT'S REALLY NICE THAT THEY LET PEOPLE TRAVELING WITH KIDS PRE-BOARD LIKE THIS.

KIRKMAN & SCOTT

I KNOW. IT'S GREAT TO HAVE A CHANCE TO GET SETTLED.

CLICK!

OKAY... YOU CAN LET EVERYBODY ELSE ON NOW.

SHHH!

QUIET: BABY ASLEEP

THEY'RE HERE!

ARRIVALS

MOM! DADDY! IT'S GREAT TO...

SWIPE!

KIRKMAN & SCOTT

...BE HERE.

OOH! TICKLE! COO! AHH! FUSS!

ARRIVALS

HOW'S IT GOING, MR. WIZOWSKI?

CALL ME HUGH! HOW'S MY GRANDSON?

IT'S YOUR GRAND **DAUGHTER**, AND SHE'S FINE, MR. WIZOWSKI.

GRAND **DAUGHTER**! WHAT DID I SAY...GRAND **SON**? WHERE'S MY **MIND**?

I'VE ASKED MYSELF THAT QUESTION FOR YEARS, **HUGH**.

CALL ME MR. WIZOWSKI.

KIRKMAN & SCOTT

THAT'S THE LAST OF IT.

WELL, I GUESS WE'RE OFFICIALLY HERE.

FOR HOW LONG?

KIRKMAN & SCOTT

WHEN YOU WERE A BABY, I ALWAYS USED CLOTH DIAPERS.

WHEN YOU WERE A BABY, BREAST-FEEDING WASN'T VERY POPULAR.

WHEN YOU WERE A BABY, I ALWAYS DRESSED YOU IN PINK.

BIG NEWS—WHEN I WAS A BABY, THE WORLD WAS PERFECT.

HERE YOU GO, WANDA.

KITCHIE KOO!

WE TICKLED, CUDDLED, DISPLAYED, INDULGED AND GENERALLY OVER-STIMULATED THE BABY.

SHE'S ALL **YOURS.** G'NIGHT.

HOW GRANDPARENTS GET EVEN.

KIRKMAN & SCOTT

SOMETIMES I WONDER IF MY MOM APPROVES OF THE WAY I TAKE CARE OF ZOE.

DOES SHE THINK I FEED HER RIGHT? DOES SHE THINK I DIAPER HER RIGHT? DOES SHE THINK I HOLD HER RIGHT?

DON'T BE SILLY, WANDA...

...OF COURSE SHE DOESN'T.

THANKS. YOU'RE A BIG HELP.

KIRKMAN & SCOTT

I'M SO TIRED I CAN'T MAKE DINNER.

I'M SO TIRED I CAN'T **EAT** DINNER.

I'M SO TIRED I CAN'T **SPELL** DINNER.

YOU WIN.

COMPETITIVE WHINING. (PARENT DIVISION.)

YOU'VE BEEN LIKE THIS FOR THREE HOURS, ZOE!

YOU WON'T GO TO SLEEP, YOU WON'T TAKE YOUR BOTTLE, AND YOU WON'T STOP FUSSING!

WHY DO YOU HAVE TO BE SO **IMMATURE**?!

BECAUSE SHE'S A **BABY**?

OH, SURE. TAKE **HER** SIDE.

I USED TO WONDER HOW PEOPLE WITH BABIES COULD GET BY ON THREE HOURS OF SLEEP A NIGHT.

BUT I'VE BEEN DOING IT FOR A FEW WEEKS NOW, AND IT'S NO BIG DEAL.

IT'S ACTUALLY PRETTY EASY. THE HUMAN BODY IS AN **AMAZING** MACHINE.

YOU JUST PUT THE MILK IN THE PANTRY AND THE CEREAL IN THE FRIDGE.

I SAID "AMAZING," NOT "PHENOMENAL."

WHAT AN ADORABLE BABY! HOW OLD IS SHE?

THREE WEEKS...

...TWO DAYS...

...TWELVE HOURS, SIXTEEN MINUTES, FORTY-FOUR SECONDS...

COLICKY, HUH?

OH, YEAH,

Z

PULLED LIGAMENTS

TENNIS ELBOW

HAIRLINE FRACTURE

TRICK KNEE

BATTLE SCARS

BEET JUICE

SPIT UP

FORMULA STAIN

BABY OIL

KIRKMAN & SCOTT

I LOVE BEING A MOMMY...

BZZZT!

...BUT THERE ARE CERTAIN THINGS I MISS ABOUT OUR LIFE BEFORE ZOE.

LIKE WHAT? THE FREEDOM? LACK OF RESPONSIBILITY? WEEKENDS OFF?

THE CHANCE TO DO SOMETHING WITH BOTH HANDS.

KIRKMAN & SCOTT

BABY BLUES®

BY RICK KIRKMAN / JERRY SCOTT

It's funny... I can't remember why we decided to use disposable diapers on Zoe.

UMPH!

KIRKMAN & SCOTT

It was the convenience.

ZOE IS ASLEEP, THE HOUSE IS RELATIVELY ORGANIZED AND IT'S ONLY 10 O'CLOCK! DO YOU **KNOW** WHAT THIS **MEANS?**

IT MEANS WE CAN ACTUALLY SPEND SOME TIME TOGETHER ALONE!

DINNER!

TV!

CONVERSATION!

ROMANCE!

Z Z

SHE'S BEEN CRYING FOR HOURS, WANDA. WHAT DO YOU THINK COULD BE WRONG?

SHHH!

THE WORLD IS A SCARY PLACE FOR BABIES. EXPERTS THINK THEY ACTUALLY LONG FOR THE WARMTH AND SECURITY OF THE IN UTERO EXPERIENCE.

SHE'S WOMB-SICK?

SOMETHING LIKE THAT.

CAN WE GO NOW?

IN A MINUTE. LOOK AT THIS TOOL.

LOOK AT THE PRECISION CRAFTING. FEEL THE BALANCE.

MAN, WOULD I LOVE TO HAVE ONE OF THESE BABIES!

WHAT DOES IT DO?

HECK IF I KNOW.

KIRKMAN & SCOTT

THIS BOOK SAYS THAT YOU SHOULD TAKE IN MORE CALORIES WHILE BREAST-FEEDING THAN DURING PREGNANCY.

I AM.

THEY MEAN **ME**, DUMMY.

KIRKMAN & SCOTT

TUESDAY

- Feed the baby
- Change the baby
- Change the baby
- Change the baby
- Feed the baby
- Change the baby
- Ignore the housework
- Change the baby
- Change the baby
- Run away to Rio (Ha! Ha! just kidding!)
- Change the baby
- Feed the baby

WANDA CHECKS HER SCHEDULE.

KIRKMAN & SCOTT

YOU'RE A VERY LUCKY GIRL, ZOE.

MOMMY AND DADDY ARE GOING TO FEED, CLOTHE, SHELTER, EDUCATE, ENTERTAIN, CHAUFFEUR AND GENERALLY TAKE CARE OF YOU UNTIL WE'RE OLD AND GREY...

KIRKMAN & SCOTT

...THEN IT'LL BE YOUR TURN.

DARRYL! YOU'RE SCARING HER!

WAAAH!

74

I THINK THE HARDEST THING TO GET USED TO AS A NEW MOTHER, IS ISOLATION.

OH, SURE, THE FATIGUE IS A PROBLEM, BUT NOT HAVING SOMEONE TO DISCUSS WORLD EVENTS WITH IS WHAT I MISS MOST ABOUT WORKING.

SIGH

SO, HOW 'BOUT THAT EASTERN EUROPE?

KIRKMAN & SCOTT

HOOSH! HOOSH! HOOSH! HOOSH! HOOOOUP!

ZIP!

FWOOOOSH!

WOW! A ONE-BREATH DIAPER CHANGE! I'M IMPRESSED!

EAT YOUR HEART OUT, JACQUES COUSTEAU!

KIRKMAN & SCOTT

SIGH

FEELING DOWN AGAIN, HONEY?

I READ SOMETHING THAT MIGHT HELP.

"ALTHOUGH NEW MOTHERS CRAVE SYMPATHY, A CLEAR UNDERSTANDING OF THE PSYCHOLOGY OF POSTPARTUM DEPRESSION IS ULTIMATELY MORE REWARDING."

SIGH

I MEAN, POOR BABY.

THAT'S BETTER.

KIRKMAN & SCOTT

BABY BLUES®

BY RICK KIRKMAN / JERRY SCOTT

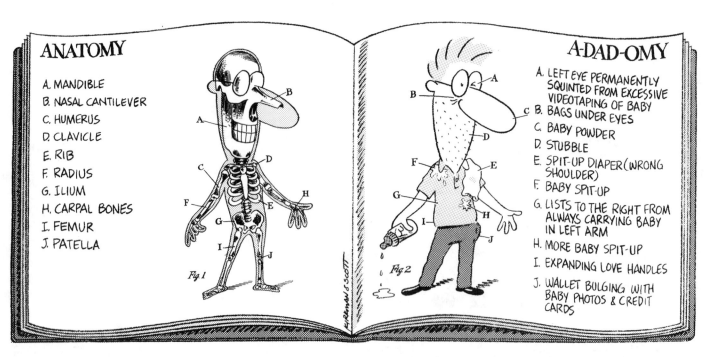

ANATOMY

A. MANDIBLE

B. NASAL CANTILEVER

C. HUMERUS

D. CLAVICLE

E. RIB

F. RADIUS

G. ILIUM

H. CARPAL BONES

I. FEMUR

J. PATELLA

Fig 1

A-DAD-OMY

A. LEFT EYE PERMANENTLY SQUINTED FROM EXCESSIVE VIDEOTAPING OF BABY

B. BAGS UNDER EYES

C. BABY POWDER

D. STUBBLE

E. SPIT-UP DIAPER (WRONG SHOULDER)

F. BABY SPIT-UP

G. LISTS TO THE RIGHT FROM ALWAYS CARRYING BABY IN LEFT ARM

H. MORE BABY SPIT-UP

I. EXPANDING LOVE HANDLES

J. WALLET BULGING WITH BABY PHOTOS & CREDIT CARDS

Fig 2

78

WANDA, I THINK WE SHOULD GO OUT FOR A NICE, ROMANTIC DINNER...

...JUST THE TWO OF US.

YEAH, ALL WE HAVE TO DO IS FIND A BABY SITTER, MAKE A SCHEDULE FOR HER TO FOLLOW, GET ALL THE BABY'S THINGS TOGETHER, CLEAN UP THE HOUSE, AND FIND SOMETHING TO WEAR!

SO...WHEN DO YOU WANT TO GO?

HOW ABOUT A YEAR FROM SATURDAY?

KIRKMAN & SCOTT

I'VE DECIDED TO ASK MY SISTER TO BABY-SIT ZOE WHILE WE GO OUT THIS WEEKEND.

RHONDA?? WHAT DOES SHE KNOW ABOUT BABIES?

NOTHING... BUT SHE'S RELIABLE, RESPONSIBLE AND CHEAP.

IF YOU SAY SO.

BESIDES, IF SHE SCREWS UP, SHE KNOWS I'LL TELL MOM.

KIRKMAN & SCOTT

HEY, RHONDA, THANKS AGAIN FOR OFFERING TO BABY-SIT.

WHAT ARE SISTERS FOR?

BEFORE WE GO, I THOUGHT WE MIGHT GO OVER A FEW THINGS THAT YOU'LL NEED TO REMEMBER ABOUT THE BABY.

OKAY. SURE.

"THIS END UP."

SHOULD I WRITE THAT DOWN?

KIRKMAN & SCOTT

THIS IS THE FIRST TIME WE'VE LEFT ZOE WITH ANYONE, SO BEAR WITH ME IF I SEEM OVERPROTECTIVE.

WANDA, I'M YOUR SISTER. I AM AN ADULT. I'M PERFECTLY CAPABLE OF CARING FOR MY NIECE FOR A FEW MEASLY HOURS WHILE YOU GO OUT TO DINNER.

BESIDES... SHE'S JUST A BABY! WHAT CAN GO WRONG?

KIRKMAN & SCOTT

I'M GLAD YOU ASKED.

BABIES

OKAY, KIDDO, YOUR FOLKS HAVE GONE. IT LOOKS LIKE IT'S JUST YOU AND YOUR AUNT RHONDA FOR THE NEXT FEW HOURS.

WHAT DO YOU WANT TO DO FIRST... WATCH A COUPLE OF OLD MOVIES? DRINK A COUPLE OF SODAS?

PHTTHT!

WAAA!

...PIERCE A COUPLE OF EARDRUMS?

SNIFF!

KIRKMAN & SCOTT

WE'RE HOME! HOW WAS SHE? DID SHE CRY? DID SHE EAT? DID SHE MISS US?

WHERE ARE YOU GOING?

TO HAVE MY TUBES TIED!

KIRKMAN & SCOTT

BABY BLUES®

BY RICK KIRKMAN / JERRY SCOTT

WHAT DO YOU SAY WE RELAX AND DO A LITTLE CUDDLING ON THE COUCH?

ARE YOU **KIDDING?** I'VE GOT A MILLION THINGS TO DO!

I APPRECIATE THE OFFER, BUT WITH THE NEW BABY, THERE JUST ISN'T TIME RIGHT NOW.

I WAS HERE FIRST!

HUSH LITTLE BABY, DON'T SAY A WORD, MOMMY'S GONNA BUY YOU A MOCKINGBIRD, AND IF THAT MOCKINGBIRD DON'T SING, MOMMY'S GONNA BUY YOU A DIAMOND RING...

I'LL GIVE YOU A HUNDRED BUCKS TO KEEP, IF YOU STOP CRYING AND LET ME SLEEP.

SAME SONG, DIFFERENT LYRICS.

FLOWERS, TREES, HONEY BEES... OOOMMM...

MANTRA

I COULD USE SOME HELP AROUND THE HOUSE... OOOMMM.

MOMTRA

KIRKMAN & SCOTT

MY NAME IS WANDA. BUT SOMEDAY YOU'LL LEARN TO TALK, AND I'LL BE "MA-MA."

AND WHEN YOU GET OLDER, YOU'LL CALL ME "MOMMY," THEN "MOM," AND THEN ONE DAY YOU'LL HAVE A BABY OF YOUR OWN AND I'LL BE "GRAM..."

"WANDA" AGAIN.

KIRKMAN & SCOTT

SMOOCH!

WHAT'S THAT FOR?

THAT'S FOR BEING A BEAUTIFUL WOMAN, A GREAT WIFE AND A TERRIFIC MOTHER.

NO, I MEAN, WHAT'S IT **FOR**? I LIKED IT, BUT I CAN'T REMEMBER WHY.

WHEN ROMANCE HAS BEEN AWAY TOO LONG.

KIRKMAN & SCOTT

IS DADDY'S WIDDLE GULL SWEEPY? IS SHE WEADY TO GO BEDDY BYE?

HUR WIDDLE EYES ARE **SOOOO** SWEEPY, AND...

...AND THE PRINCESS LEAPT ONTO HER SHINY BLACK HORSE AND GALLOPED AWAY TOWARD...

AWE WOO DADDY'S WIDDLE GULL? YES, YOU **ARE**!

KIRKMAN & SCOTT

84

EXERCISE

WHIRR
WHIRR
WHIRR

JAZZERCISE

MOMERCISE

IT'S SO WEIRD.
WHAT?

PARENTHOOD. IT'S ALMOST IMPOSSIBLE TO DESCRIBE.

IT'S FASCINATING... IT'S EXCITING... IT'S CAPTIVATING... IT'S... IT'S...

MORE DIFFICULT THAN YOU EVER IMAGINED IN YOUR WILDEST DREAMS?
YOU NOTICED THAT, TOO?

AW WOO DADDUM'S WIDDLE GUHL? HMM?

DAR-RYL!!

I THOUGHT WE AGREED NOT TO TALK "BABY TALK" TO ZOE.

SOWWY.

THAT'S *NOT* FUNNY!

I'M NOT TWYIN' TO BE FUNNY! I'M 'TUCK! I CAN'T 'TOP TAWKIN' BABY TAWK!

WHAT???

I KNEW IF I CWOSSED MY EYES FO' TOO WONG DEY'D 'TICK, BUT I NEVUH 'SPECTED DIS!

I *TOLD* YOU NOT TO TALK "BABY TALK" TO ZOE, AND NOW LOOK WHAT HAPPENED!

I KNOW! I CAN'T 'TOP! WOTTA WE GONNA DO?

HOW SHOULD I KNOW? I'VE NEVER HEARD OF THIS...ARE YOU *SURE* YOU CAN'T STOP?

DA WAIN IN 'PAIN FAWS MAINWY ON DA PWAIN.

GREAT! YOU SOUND LIKE A TWO-YEAR-OLD MICHAEL CAINE.

WEX HAWISSON.

WHATEVER.

"BEING STUCK IN 'BABY TALK' IS NOT UNUSUAL. IT HAPPENS TO MANY FIRST-TIME PARENTS AND GRANDPARENTS."

YOU MEAN, I'M NOT AWONE?

APPARENTLY NOT... "THIS CONDITION IS BROUGHT ON BY THE OVERWHELMING CUTENESS OF A NEW BABY...,"

I CAN WELATE.

"...SUCCESSFUL TREATMENT OF THIS CONDITION CONSISTS OF REPEATED EXPOSURE TO A BABY DURING PEAK UN-CUTE PERIODS."

WOT'S DAT 'POSED TO MEAN?

IT MEANS YOU GET THE NIGHT SHIFT, TWEETY-BIRD.

HEY, Y'KNOW SUMPING? I TINK I'M STAWTING TO SNAP OUTTA IT!

BABY BLUES®

BY RICK KIRKMAN / JERRY SCOTT

IT'S AMAZING HOW YOUR EXPECTATIONS CHANGE AS YOUR LIFE CHANGES.

WHEN WE WERE SINGLE, I USED TO LOVE IT WHEN DARRYL WOULD TAKE ME TO FANCY RESTAURANTS.

MUNCH MUNCH **MUNCH** MUNCH

THEN, AFTER WE WERE MARRIED, I WOULD PLAN LONG, ROMANTIC DINNERS AT HOME.

NOW I'D BE HAPPY JUST TO EAT SITTING DOWN.

HAVE YOU NOTICED ZOE'S HAIR IS FALLING OUT ON TOP?

IT'S NOT FALLING OUT. IT'S JUST RUBBING OFF.

WHEN SHE SCOOTS UP TO THE CORNER OF HER CRIB, SHE RUBS THE TOP OF HER HEAD ON THE PAD, AND IT MAKES A LITTLE BALD SPOT.

CLICK!

I THINK IT MAKES HER LOOK ABSOLUTELY ADORABLE.

I THINK IT MAKES HER LOOK LIKE WILLARD SCOTT.

DEGREES

R.N.   M.D.   Ph.D.   D.A.D.

PACKING AWAY HER MATERNITY CLOTHES GIVES WANDA MIXED FEELINGS.

BABY BLUES®

BY RICK KIRKMAN / JERRY SCOTT

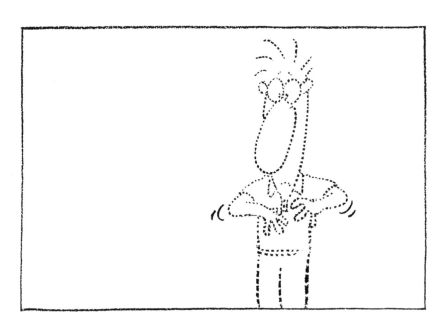

KIRKMAN & SCOTT

I **HATE** THIS!

By the time we pay our bills and taxes, there's never any money left!

Our generation is getting a raw deal, and it's time to get together and do what we do best!

Become politically active?

No, whine until we get our way.

~SIGH~

What's wrong?

Nothing... it's just that...

...I realized we have more money invested in baby products than in both of our IRAs combined!

Can you believe it? Zoe is only six weeks old and she's already smiling at us!

Travis did that at four weeks.

Not only that, Travis held his head up at five weeks.

HA! Zoe did that at four-and-a-half weeks!

ONE-UPSMOMSHIP

97

BABY BLUES®

RICK BY JERRY
KIRKMAN / SCOTT

GUESS WHAT. MY PARENTS ARE COMING FOR A VISIT.

ZIP!

TIME'S A-WASTING!

KIRKMAN & SCOTT

ARE YOU IMPLYING THAT MY MOM IS CRITICAL OF YOUR HOUSEKEEPING?

CAN'T TALK NOW... I'M DUSTING THE ICE CUBES!

ZIP!

COME ON, WANDA... MY PARENTS ARE COMING TO SEE **ZOE**, NOT TO CRITICIZE OUR HOUSEKEEPING.

TRUE OR FALSE... YOUR MOTHER ALPHABETIZES THE FOOD IN HER REFRIGERATOR?

TRUE.

I REST MY CASE.

ACTUALLY, ONLY THE **FROZEN** FOOD IS ALPHABETIZED... ALL THE OTHER STUFF IS ON THE DEWEY DECIMAL SYSTEM.

KIRKMAN & SCOTT

MOM!

DARRYL!

YOU LOOK **GREAT!** YOU, TOO! IT'S SO GOOD TO SEE YOU! HAVE YOU LOST WEIGHT? THE HOUSE IS **BEAUTIFUL!** WHERE'S THE BATHROOM? **KISS!** KISS! WHERE'S ZOE? **KISS! KISS!** SHE'S NAPPING! KISS! KISS!

DAD!

H'LO!

A NINE-HOUR CAR TRIP AND HE SAYS "H'LO"? ISN'T THAT KIND OF STRANGE?

YEAH... HE'S USUALLY NOT THIS CHATTY.

KIRKMAN & SCOTT

HERE'S A LITTLE SOMETHING FOR ZOE.

OH, PAULINE... YOU SHOULDN'T HAVE!

I MADE IT MYSELF IN CRAFTS CLASS.

OH, PAULINE... YOU SHOULDN'T HAVE!

IT'S A BAPTISMAL DRESS MADE OUT OF THOSE PLASTIC SIX-PACK RINGS.

OH, PAULINE... YOU REALLY, **REALLY** SHOULDN'T HAVE..

HEY! WATERPROOF! GOOD THINKING, MOM!

NEED SOME HELP WITH DINNER, HONEY?

NO, THANKS. WHY DON'T YOU GO CATCH UP ON THINGS WITH YOUR DAD?

SO, HOW'S IT GOING?

SAME.

GOOD, YOU?

OKAY. WE'RE DONE.

I'D FORGOTTEN HOW QUIET YOUR DAD IS.

YEAH.

HE'S THE STRONG, SILENT TYPE. A MAN OF FEW WORDS. THAT'S JUST THE WAY HE IS.

IZZAT POPPIE'S ZOE? YEZ IT IS! YOU WANT TO GO FOR A WALK? OOPIE WOOPIE BOOPIE DOOPIE! HI, MOMMY AND DADDY! BYE, MOMMY AND DADDY!

CORRECTION: THAT'S JUST THE WAY HE **WAS.**

Panel 1: MOM! YOU DON'T HAVE TO COOK... YOU'RE A GUEST!
I WAS JUST FIXING YOUR FATHER'S BREAKFAST.

Panel 2: IT'S HIS FAVORITE... DECAFFEINATED COFFEE, ARTIFICIAL SWEETENER, SCRAMBLED EGG SUBSTITUTE, MEATLESS BACON AND ORANGE-FLAVORED BREAKFAST DRINK.

Panel 3: WANT SOME?
NO, THANKS. I'M ON A LOW-PLASTIC DIET.
IS SOMEONE FRYING LINOLEUM?

Panel 4: UH-OH... SHE WANTS GRANDMA TO FEED HER!

Panel 5: UH-OH... SHE WANTS GRANDMA TO CHANGE HER!

Panel 6: UH-OH... SHE WANTS GRANDMA TO ROCK HER!

Panel 7: UH-OH... SHE WANTS GRANDMA TO COOL IT.

Panel 8: MOM! IT'S ONLY 6:30! HOW LONG HAVE YOU BEEN UP?
NOT LONG.

Panel 9: JUST LONG ENOUGH TO STRIP AND WAX THE KITCHEN FLOOR, REORGANIZE THE CUPBOARDS AND POLISH THE SILVERWARE.

Panel 10: YOU NEVER CHANGE, MOM... I'M GOING BACK TO BED.
IF I GET BORED LATER, IS IT OKAY IF I RELANDSCAPE THE YARD?

KIRKMAN & SCOTT

BABY BLUES®

RICK KIRKMAN / JERRY SCOTT BY

FAMILY PORTRAIT #1

THE SECRET TO GOOD FAMILY RELATIONSHIPS IS FOR ALL PARTIES TO SHARE A COMMON INTEREST.

KIRKMAN & SCOTT

COME ON, ZOE, IT'S TIME TO GET DRESSED.

N-N-N-NO!!

YOUR DADDY ALWAYS HATES TO SEE YOU LEAVE.

ESPECIALLY WHEN IT'S WITH TWO FISTFULS OF CHEST HAIR!

KIRKMAN & SCOTT

BEFORE PARENTHOOD...

WE'D BETTER GET READY TO GO. THE MOVIE STARTS IN ABOUT TEN MINUTES.

AFTER PARENTHOOD...

WE'D BETTER GET READY TO GO. THE MOVIE STARTS IN ABOUT TEN HOURS.

KIRKMAN & SCOTT

UH-OH... YOU'RE WET, ZOE.

HANG ON, KIDDO! I'LL CHANGE YOUR DIAPER JUST AS SOON AS WE GET THROUGH THE...

...CHECKOUT.

I WONDER WHAT SHE WANTS?

I THINK SHE'S TRYING TO SAY THAT SHE'S HUNGRY.

I WONDER WHAT SHE WANTS NOW?

I THINK SHE'S TRYING TO SAY THAT SHE WANTS TO BE ROCKED.

I WONDER WHAT SHE WANTS *NOW*?

I THINK SHE'S TRYING TO DRIVE US CRAZY.

OKAY... ARE WE READY TO GO TO THE PARK?

YEAH, I THINK THAT'S EVERYTHING.

HATS... SUNSCREEN... COOLER... BLANKET... JACKETS... UMBRELLA...

SOMETHING WRONG?

WE'VE NOT ONLY BECOME PARENTS, WE'VE BECOME NERDS!

THE QUARTERBACK TAKES THE SNAP! HE FADES BACK!

IT'S A PASS!

NO... IT'S A SWEEP! NO...

BONK!

CRASH!

IT'S A QUARTERBACK SNEAK.

WHAT WAS THAT NOISE?

KIRKMAN & SCOTT

IT'S FOUR O'CLOCK IN THE MORNING AND WE'RE SITTING HERE WITH THIS ☆@#¢! SCREAMING KID.

WHAT COULD BE WORSE THAN **THIS**?

SITTING HERE **WITHOUT** THIS ☆@#¢! SCREAMING KID.

THANKS, I NEEDED THAT.

YOU'RE WELCOME.

KIRKMAN & SCOTT

man-hour (măn′owr′) n. the amount of work that a man can do in one hour.

BEEP! BEEP!

CLICK!

mom-hour (mŏm′owr′) n. equal to at least ten man-hours.

WHIRRRR!

KIRKMAN & SCOTT

WILDLIFE PHOTOGRAPHER

CHILDLIFE PHOTOGRAPHER

KIRKMAN & SCOTT

WHAT A **GREAT** MOVIE!

BADA: DANCE

LAMBA THE FORBID

ARE YOU **KIDDING?** THAT HAD TO BE THE **WORST** FILM OF THE YEAR!

DUMB PLOT, STEREOTYPED CHARACTERS, BAD ACTORS... HOW CAN YOU SAY IT WAS **GREAT**?!

ANY MOVIE THAT GETS YOU AWAY FROM A COLICKY TWO-MONTH-OLD BABY FOR TWO-AND-A-HALF HOURS IS A GREAT MOVIE.

AMEN.

MAYBE YOU SHOULD START CARRYING ZOE IN THE OTHER ARM FOR AWHILE.

KIRKMAN & SCOTT

BABY BLUES®

BY RICK KIRKMAN / JERRY SCOTT

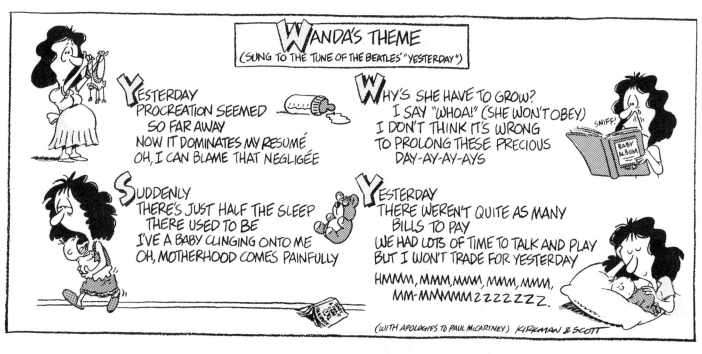

BING-BONG

DARRYL! WANDA! WHAT A SURPRISE!

HI. WE CAN ONLY STAY A MINUTE.

DID NOT! DID NOT! DID NOT! DID **NOT**!

DID, TOO! DID, TOO! DID, TOO! DID, **TOO**!

WAAAA!

did not
did not
did not

did, too
did, too
did, too

① IS SHE GETTING ENOUGH TO EAT?

② ARE WE PAYING ENOUGH ATTENTION TO HER?

COLIC? FOUR QUESTIONS TO ASK

IS SHE COMFORTABLE? ③

④ WHOSE IDEA WAS THIS, ANYWAY?

WE NEED A NEW CAR.

UH-OH...

THIS ONE IS TOO SMALL, NOW THAT WE HAVE ZOE.

DON'T SAY IT.

WE NEED A CAR WITH LOTS OF CARGO SPACE FOR ALL THE BABY STUFF WE HAUL AROUND. LET'S FACE IT... WE NEED A...

PLEASE... DON'T USE THE S-WORD!

...STATION WAGON.

AAAGGH!

KIRKMAN & SCOTT

I DON'T UNDERSTAND YOUR AVERSION TO OWNING A STATION WAGON, DARRYL.

UNH!

PORTA-CRIB

IT'S SIMPLE. A STATION WAGON IS A STATEMENT.

KIRKMAN & SCOTT

A STATION WAGON SAYS YOU'RE SETTLED... IT SAYS YOU'RE BORING... IT SAYS YOU'VE GIVEN UP!

IT SAYS YOU GOT TIRED OF HAULING 300 CUBIC FEET OF BABY JUNK STRAPPED TO THE ROOF OF YOUR CAR.

I KNOW! HOW ABOUT A MIATA WITH A TRAILER HITCH?

I CAN'T BELIEVE THAT YOU STILL THINK WE DON'T NEED A NEW CAR, DARRYL.

JUST IMAGINE THAT NEW CAR FEEL. JUST IMAGINE THAT NEW CAR SMELL. JUST IMAGINE THAT NEW CAR PRESTIGE.

BIG DEAL. SO WHAT? WHO CARES?

JUST IMAGINE HAVING ROOM TO FIT ZOE'S CAR SEAT BACK THERE.

TAKE A LEFT AT THE CORNER. THERE'S A DEALERSHIP ON YOUR RIGHT.

WELCOME TO **WAGON WORLD!** HOW CAN I HELP YOU FOLKS?

WE'RE LOOKING FOR A BIGGER CAR.

SOMETHING ROOMY... BUT NOT **TOO** ROOMY, SENSIBLE... BUT NOT **TOO** SENSIBLE, ECONOMICAL... BUT NOT **TOO** ECONOMICAL...

KIRKMAN & SCOTT

FIRST FAMILY CAR?

BE GENTLE.

DO THEY COME WITH RACING STRIPES OR ANYTHING?

THE AUTO-MAKERS UNDERSTAND YOUR AVERSION TOWARD FAMILY CARS

WAGON WORL

THEY KNOW THAT PEOPLE IN YOUR AGE GROUP DON'T WANT TO DRIVE THE SAME CARS THAT YOUR PARENTS DID.

THAT'S WHY WE HAVE RESPONDED TO YOUR DESIRES WITH A RADICALLY NEW CONCEPT IN AUTOMOTIVE MARKETING.

KIRKMAN & SCOTT

YOU'VE STOPPED MAKING STATION WAGONS?

NOPE. WE STARTED CALLING THEM SPORT UTILITY VEHICLES!

NOW LET ME SEE IF I HAVE THIS STRAIGHT...

YOU FOLKS ARE LOOKING FOR A CAR THAT'S ROOMY YET SPORTY... SENSIBLE YET DARING AND LUXURIOUS YET SIMPLE.

RIGHT.

I HAVE JUST THE CAR YOU FOLKS ARE LOOKING FOR... THE 1991 OXYMORON!

SO, WHAT DO YOU THINK?

IMPRESSIVE YET DISAPPOINTING.

I KNEW YOU'D LIKE IT.

KIRKMAN & SCOTT

WHAT'S TAKING HIM SO LONG?

HE'S INSPECTING OUR TRADE-IN.

UH-OH.

I KNOW, HE'S BOUND TO SEE THE LEAKY TRANSMISSION, BALD TIRES AND THE DENT IN THE DOOR,

LET'S FACE IT... IT'S A PIECE OF JUNK.

OKAY, FOLKS... HERE'S HOW MUCH WE CAN GIVE YOU FOR YOUR TRADE-IN.

ARE YOU **CRAZY??** FOR THAT LITTLE **CREAMPUFF?**

SIXTEEN-FIVE.

SIXTEEN-NINE!

SIXTEEN-FIVE.

SIXTEEN-NINE!

?

WAAAA

OKAY! OKAY! IT'S A **DEAL!** SIXTEEN-**FIVE!**

AND A FREE CD PLAYER.

I CAN'T BELIEVE WE BOUGHT A NEW CAR! THIS IS **SO** EXCITING!

I JUST LOVE IT! THE COLOR IS PERFECT, THE SEATS ARE COMFORTABLE AND THERE'S NOTHING LIKE THAT NEW CAR SMELL!

I BET WITHIN A MONTH OR SO YOU'LL EVEN GET OVER YOUR EMBARRASSMENT ABOUT DRIVING A STATION WAGON.

YEAH, RIGHT.

BABY BLUES

RICK KIRKMAN / JERRY SCOTT BY

THUP! THUP! THUP! THUP! THUP! THUP! THUP! THUP!

Babies Who Suck Too Much & The Moms Who Let Them

YOU KNOW, THIS SAYS THAT PACIFIERS AREN'T A VERY GOOD IDEA.

IT SAYS THAT IF A BABY ALWAYS HAS A PACIFIER, IT WILL KEEP HER FROM EXPLORING TOYS AND OTHER OBJECTS WITH HER MOUTH, WHICH IS AN IMPORTANT PART OF HER DEVELOPMENT.

ACCORDING TO THIS, YOU SHOULD TAKE IT AWAY BEFORE THE BABY BECOMES TOO ATTACHED TO IT.

TOO LATE.

YOU'RE GOING TO BE GONE ALL DAY??

PROBABLY, I NEED TO DO SOME SERIOUS SHOPPING.

AND I'LL BE HERE TAKING CARE OF ZOE ALL BY MYSELF?

YOU'LL BE FINE. IT'LL GIVE YOU A CHANCE TO HONE YOUR PARENTING SKILLS.

HEY, I JUST BECAME A **DADDY**! I'M NOT QUALIFIED TO BE A **PARENT**!

CONSIDER THIS A BATTLEFIELD PROMOTION.

SMACK!

KIRKMAN & SCOTT

BYE, HONEY! MOMMY WILL BE BACK THIS AFTERNOON!

JUST SEVEN HOURS OR SO.

KISS! KISS! KISS! KISS!

CLICK!

SIX HOURS, FIFTY-NINE MINUTES, FORTY-FIVE SECONDS OR SO... SIX HOURS, FIFTY-NINE MINUTES, FORTY-FOUR SECONDS OR SO...

AAAAA!

KIRKMAN & SCOTT

WHAT ARE YOU DOING?

IF YOU'RE GOING TO BE GONE SHOPPING ALL DAY, I NEED TO HAVE MY ACT TOGETHER.

LET'S SEE...FORMULA, BOTTLES, PACIFIER, FEED, BURP, DIAPER, BATHE, DRESS, ROCK... UH-OH...

FORGET SOMETHING?

YEAH.

I CAN TAKE CARE OF ZOE, BUT WHO'S GOING TO TAKE CARE OF ME?

KIRKMAN & SCOTT

124